Distributed by Scholastic, Inc.
90 Old Sherman Turnpike
Danbury, CT 06816

Published by
The Child's World, Inc.
7081 West 192nd Ave.
Eden Prairie, Minnesota 55346

Here Comes the Big Parade

My First Steps to Reading Treasury

by Jane Belk Moncure
illustrated by Linda Hohag

Clap your hands. Tap your feet.
A parade is coming down the street.

Little

and the alligator lead the way.
"You can come along too," they say.

"First let's stop and do the alligator hop.

Hop like a bunny and a little

kangaroo.

Walk like an elephant in the zoo."

7

Aa

"Fly like a butterfly.   Swim like a   whale.

Be a little puppy.   Chase your tail."

"Be a little top. Spin all around.

Bend down to the ground.

Good for you," they say as they hop away.

Here comes Little **b** with baby baboon

and bear on a bicycle with a balloon.

"Today is my birthday," says the little bear.
"I have a bottle of bubbles to share."

10

"Thanks," says bird.

"This is fun.

I can blow bubbles one by one."

"Thanks," says bunny.
"Look what I can do.

I can blow bubbles two by two."

11

Bb

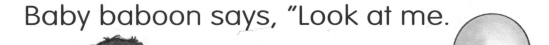

Baby baboon says, "Look at me.

I can blow bubbles three by three."

Little bear says, "I can do more.

I can blow bubbles
four by four."

UBBLES

12

Little bear blows.

The bubble grows and goes *pop!*

Little **b** says,

"Now let's stop."

13

Here comes Little C with the cat and the clown.

"Hi," he says, jumping up and down.
"Come and clown around with me.
Are you ready? One, two, three."

"Wiggle your fingers.

Pinch your nose.

Make a funny face.

Touch your toes."

"Be a tree.   Sway your branches around.

Shake your leaves down to the ground.

Good," says Little .

16

"Now rhyme a rhyme with me.

What word rhymes with

snake,

lake,

and rake?

What do you put in the oven to bake?

Is it little bear's birthday ?"

"Yes," say clown and Little .

"Do you have any cake for me?"

asks Little Dd. Here she comes with

a duck, a dog, and a dancing dinosaur.
"I will wind him up so he will dance for you."

Oops! The dinosaur

dances very fast.

Away he goes.

"Stop," cries Little

But the dinosaur keeps dancing.

19

Dd

The dog and the duck
try to catch him.

But the dinosaur keeps dancin

until he gets dizzy…

...and falls into a ditch.

Little  picks him up.

"Next time I shall not wind you up so tight."

Next comes Little e on the elephant's back.

The elves are carrying a great big sack.

"Guess what is in the sack?" says Little e.

"Let's open the sack and see."

"Hooray," say the elves. "We can exercise today.

We can jump, skip, and do a flip.

We can bat the ball. We can catch...

Ee

...and throw.

Exercise helps us grow and grow.

So swing

and jump.

"Slide down a slide.

Hop on your bike and take a ride.

Exercise is fun, fun, fun. It is good for everyone."

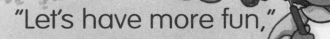

"Let's have more fun," says Little f. "Come, play a finger game with me. Hold up your fingers, one, two, three.

Three frogs go fishing in a little canoe."

"One jumps after a big fat fly.
That leaves two.

Two little frogs sit in the sun.
One jumps into the fish pond.
That leaves one.

Along comes a hungry fox.
'Splash' goes the frog.
That leaves none.

Bye-bye,"
and away they run.

Ff

27

"What a fun day for me,"

says Little

"Come and see my   gorillas

and goats

all dressed up in hats and coats,
with green umbrellas and high-heeled shoes."

"Giggling and dancing two by two.

If you like to giggle, join the fun.

Giggles are good for everyone."

Gg

"I giggle when I tell secrets
to a silly clown.

I giggle when he does a flip

and tumbles

upside down."

"I giggle when I dance a jig
with a pig
in a yellow wig.

Giggles keep you smiling,
so giggle while you play.
Have a happy giggle time
every day," says Little   as she skips away.

Next comes Little h and hippo.

He will tell you the story
about his hat.
"I wore my hat right-side up
until I met horse.
He said, 'Hee-haw,
what a funny hat.'"

Hh

h

"Then I met  hog. He said, 'Ha-ha, what a funny hat.'

I was not happy with my hat after that.

I hopped into a hammock and went to sleep.

While I was sleeping, hen came by."

33

Hh

"She did not say 'Hee-haw' or 'Ha-ha.' She said, 'Hip, hip hooray,

what a fine henhouse for my chicks and me.'

I am so glad to have hen for my friend that I wear my hat upside down."

'Now horse does not say 'Hee-haw.'
Hog does not say 'Ha-ha.'

Hen and her chicks are happy."

"We are all happy," says Little as they hop away.

"It is time for a rest,"

says Little

"I have ice cream cones and ice cream pie.

Stop a minute for a tasty treat.
Come and taste my ice cream, nice and sweet."

"Come and taste chocolate, vanilla,

peach and cherry, lemon, orange, and sweet strawberry."

As Little

skips along,

she sings her happy ice cream song.

"I like ice cream at the circus,

in the park,

and at the zoo.

I like ice cream on

a boat

or a train

and in an airplane too

"I like ice cream in the springtime and all the year through.

I like ice cream at a
birthday party best of all
with you."

"I like ice cream too," says Little

"I have a game
everyone can play.
It is called jack-in-the-box."

Little j was hiding in a box.
He was very still and quiet

until a little boy saw the box...

and started to untie it.
When he opened up the top
The jack-in-the-box went
pop!

Now little  jumps away.

J j

41

Jj

Next comes Little with kittens and kangaroo.

Kangaroo can count all the kittens in her pocket. Can you?

Kangaroo can share her things:

toys and blocks,

see-saw,

and swings.

43

Kk

Kangaroo
makes up her bed

and puts her toys away.

She helps to take care of her sister
on a rainy day.

44

She rocks her to sleep and hugs her too.
"I love my sister," says Kangaroo.

"We try to be helpful
and kind each day,"

says Little

as they march away.

"I want to be kind,"

says Little 1.

"Guess what I can do?
I can share my lollipops with you
Take one, two, or three.
What colors will they be?

The lambs have yellow,   green,   and blue."

46

"The lion has orange and purple ones, too.

The leopard has red ones,

the lobster has brown.

I have the best lollipops in town."

47

Ll

Little **m** and the monkeys sa

"Guess what we can do?

We can rhyme three special words with you.

The first word rhymes with trees,

48

 bees,

 keys,

 chimpanzees, and cheese.

The special word is **_please_**."

Mm

"The second word rhymes with piggy banks

and little fish tanks.

The special word is *thanks*."

"The third special word rhymes with  starry.

It shines really bright when we say *sorry.*"

Little **m** says,

"These special words can turn a frown right-side up from upside down."

"These special words are very nice.
They shine like stars," say the little mice.

please   **thanks**   **sorry**

"We say *'please'* when we want more cheese."

The monkeys say, "When we fuss or fight,

we say *'sorry'* to make things right."

"We all say *'thanks'* for this summer day,"

says Little

as they march away.

Here comes Little

"Guess what I can

do?" she says.

"I can read **My Number Book** to you.

I know my house number and the name of my street."

"I know my telephone number.

999-9029

I have three pets.

3 pets

1 - Sunday
2 - Monday
3 - Tuesday
4 - Wednesday
5 - Thursday
6 - Friday
7 - Saturday

I can count nine coins in my bank.

9 coins

I can count the days in the week.

I can do more," says Little n.

Nn

"I can put number word puzzles together. Can you?"

6 six

7 seven

8 eight

9 nine

10 ten

"I can count up to ten and down again,"

says Little

and away she goes.

Norman

Next comes Little to play with you.

He says, "Guess what my octopus can do?

He can make lots of **o**'s for you.

I can make **o** pictures too."

"One **o** can be a happy face,

a moon, a clock, a ball.

One orange **o** can be a jack-o-lantern, big or small.

Two **o**'s can be an owl's two eyes

or glasses that you wear."

Oo

"Three **o**'s can be a snowman in the frosty winter air.

Three **o**'s can be tricycle wheels, or a big bright

traffic light,

or three pancakes

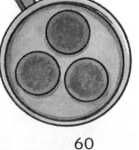

in a pan before I take a bite."

"Four **o**'s can be

four round wheels on a wagon,

a van, and an automobile.

A big **o** is a circle,"

says Little as they go away.

Along comes Little 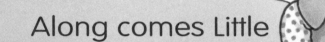 with her piglet pals.

"Guess what we will do?
We will have a puppet show for you.
Let's make puppets with paper bags, and glue." paper, scissors,

"This is how we will make paper bag puppets of

hens,

a pony,

a lamb,   and   a cow."

Pp

"The piglets will help me put on this show.
Are you ready?
Here we go.

Come with us to the farm today to see the animals at play.

"I can help you," says
cow with a moo.

"I give you milk.
That is what I do."

"Milk makes good food for you.

Milk helps your bones grow big and strong
so you can run and play all day long."

The hens say, "Cluck, cluck.   We help you too.

We lay lots of
eggs for you."

"Baa-baa," says the lamb. "I have warm wool to share with you

Wool makes sweaters and mittens too."

66

The pony says, "Neigh-neigh.

You can ride me everyday."
"Hooray for the

pony,   the hens,   the lamb, and   the cow.

Now all the animals take a bow."

"I can make puppets too"
says Little

"My queen bee puppets fit on my fingers.
They have words on their wings for you."

Queen bee kind.   Queen bee nice.

Queen bee honest.

Queen bee loving.

Queen bee happy.

"Both queens and kings can be this way, and so can you," says Little q as she skips away.

Qq

Little  has a surprise for you.

It is a robot.

Guess what it can do?

It can rhyme words. You can too.

Little **r** asks, "What word rhymes with train, plane, chain, and crane?"

Robot flashes this word: **rain**.

71

Rr

"Good," says Little 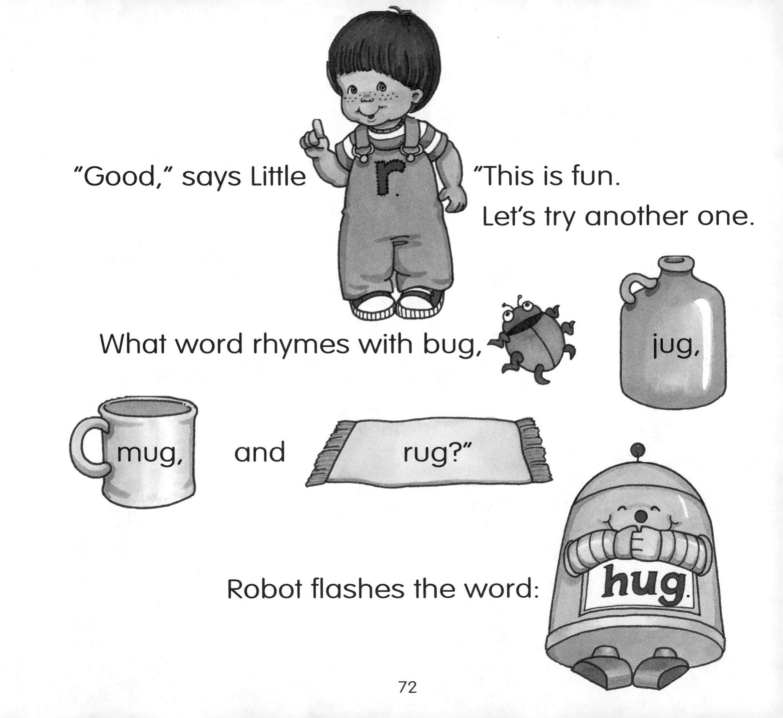 r. "This is fun. Let's try another one.

What word rhymes with bug, jug,

mug, and rug?"

Robot flashes the word: hug.

"Can you rhyme one more time? What word rhymes with

hop,

mop, top, and lollipop?"

Robot flashes: stop.

bye-bye

"Now we must stop," and away they hop.

73

Little skips along
with the seals
singing a safety song.
"Stop, Look, Listen

before we cross the street."

"When I hop into a car,

I buckle up my seat.

I wear a helmet

when I ride my bike."

75

Ss

"I wear my boots
when I go for a hike.

I am careful when I climb the   jungle gym."

"I take along my friends when I go for a swim.

Stay safe every day," says Little as he skips away.

Here comes Little

with a wagon full of trees.

"I will plant them one by one.
Come along and join the fun."

"A tree may be a home for   a bird

or a bee,

a squirrel

an owl,

or a chimpanzee."

79

Tt

"A tree may be full of oranges or pears.

A tree has wood for tables and chairs."

"A tree has wood for

toys and blocks,

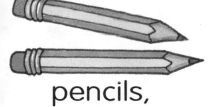

pencils,

puzzles,

and
cuckoo clocks.

A tree makes a tree house
where we can play. So plant
a tree some sunny day."

"Oh, dear, it is raining.
I know what we can do,"

says Little

"Take a rainy-day walk with me.
You never know what you will see."

"Look under these rocks.

Do you see holes

for ants   and bugs,

worms   and moles?"

83

"Look under this big log by the road.

Do you see a chipmunk, a mouse, and a toad?"

"Look under the bridge by the lake. Do you see a fish, a turtle, a frog, a snake?

The rain has stopped.
Put the umbrella away.
We can take a walk another rainy day."

Here comes

Little  with a valentine tree.

"I have valentine critters
just for you.
You can make some too."

"Make them small,

long,

or tall.

They can swim,

fly   or   crawl.

I like valentines best of all."

Vv

"I like star wishes.
Do you?"

Asks Little

"These are wishing stars," she says.
"Some wishes come true."

"The little caterpillar wished for wings. One day her wish came true.

A little tadpole wished for legs. One day his wish came true.

A little chick wished for a crown. One day his wish came true.

Here is a wishing star for you."

Ww

Is this the end of the parade with

Little **X** **Y** and **Z** ?

"No. Not yet," says Little **Z**.
"Come along and follow me."

"We will all *zoom* to your house...

Letter Kids' Express

Xx, Yy, Zz

...to make words with you."

"That is what the Letter Kids do."